Table of Contents

✷ INDICATES A REPRODUCIBLE STUDENT ACTIVITY PAGE

King David

Travel Back to Ancient Israel

Before you begin a study of the ancient Israelites with your students, tell them there has been a late-breaking news story. Rumors have it that at a certain secret place in the country of Israel, reporters are gathering. People say that at midnight tomorrow, the gathered reporters will be secretly transported back almost four thousand years. There, the reporters will actually get to find out what really happened during the life and times of the ancient Israelites.

Tell the students that in order to be eligible to go on this time trip, they must be prepared to get their reporter's credentials in order. They will need to get a press pass to identify them as reporters for their trip. Once everything is ready, they will be ready to travel to Israel to join the other reporters in a story that will prove to be a reporter's "scoop of a lifetime."

When the students return, they will be able to produce a one-of-a-kind newspaper describing their experiences in the ancient world.

Where in the Ancient World Are We?

Use the student activity sheet *Map of Ancient Israel* on page 3 to have students explore ancient Israel and the countries and bodies of water around it. As students read, discuss, and learn more about the ancient Israelites, have them fill in the map and refer to it during their discussions.

Get a Press Pass

Use the student activity sheet *Get a Press Pass* on page 4 to help students get the press pass they will need to visit ancient Israel. Encourage students to discuss the various ways of getting and processing information listed on their Press Pass Application. Have them give examples of when each type of activity would be useful in producing a newspaper or video report.

Use the Press Pass

After students have filled out their press passes, have them affix a photo or self-portrait of themselves to it. Have students fold their press passes vertically on the dotted line, and tape or laminate them. Students can then punch a hole in the press passes and use a string to wear the passes around their necks. Tell students they will need to wear the press passes when they are acting as reporters. As students explore each topic, have them check off the topic on their press passes.

Map of Ancient Israel

Name ______________________

On the map below, label the following places:

Kingdom of Israel
Syria (Aram)
Syrian Desert
Kingdom of Judah
Jerusalem
Assyrian Empire
Egypt
Mediterranean Sea
Red Sea
Gulf of Aqaba
Nazareth
Megiddo
Sinai Peninsula
Dead Sea
Gulf of Suez

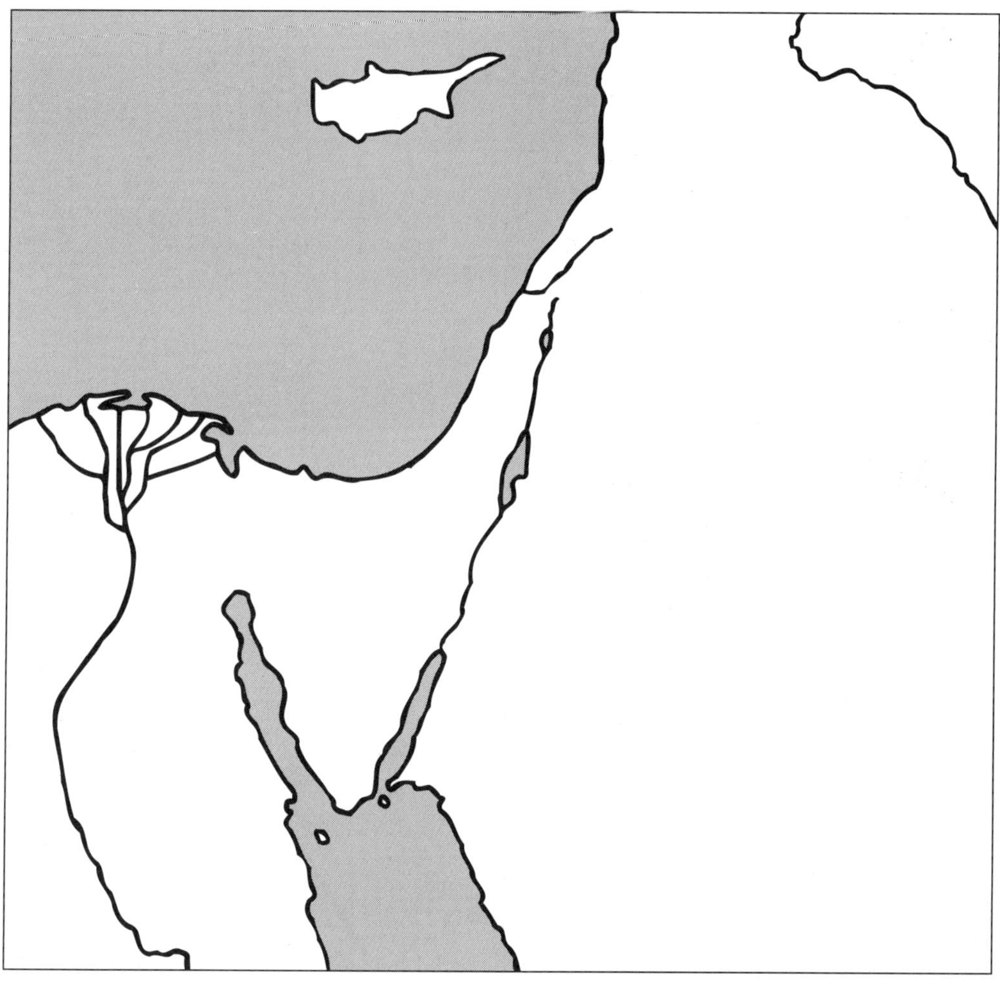

Compare this map to a modern map of this area. What has stayed the same? What has changed?

____

____

____

____

Get a Press Pass

Name ____________________

In order to be among the reporters traveling back to ancient Israel, you must have a valid press pass. Think about how you want to do your reporting as you fill out the following application.

Press Pass Application

Name (last name first) ____________________

Address ____________________

____

Date of Birth ____________ Nationality ____________

School ____________________

Number of years you have attended school ____________

Circle the types or phases of reporting you can do:

interviewing	writing an article	writing an opinion
researching	proofreading	comparing and contrasting
taking notes for a story	editing	sorting beliefs from facts

State in one sentence one or more facts that you hope to uncover while covering this story.

____

____

____

Signature ____________________

Press Pass to Ancient Israel

Name ______________________________

Name ______________________________
Address ______________________________
____
City______________________________
State ________________Zip ____________
Date of Birth ______________________________
Nationality ______________________________
Name of Newspaper or TV Network ____
____
Country Visiting ______________________________
Purpose of Visit ______________________________
____
____
____
____
____
____

Paste picture or self-portrait here

Check as each topic is investigated.

Topics

___ Polytheism and Monotheism
___ The Habiru People
___ The Bible as a Historic Source
___ The Crossing of the Red Sea
___ Wandering in the Wilderness
___ The Ten Commandments
___ Everyday Life in Ancient Israel
___ Food of the Ancient Israelites
___ Music of the Ancient Israelites
___ The First Temple
___ The Diaspora

People

___ Abraham
___ Isaac
___ Jacob
___ Moses
___ Joshua
___ Saul
___ David
___ Solomon
___ Nebuchadnezzar

Reporter's Packet

Tell students that before they go on their trip to meet the ancient Israelites as reporters, they must be armed with solid background information. In order to understand the importance of Abraham's declaration of one god, they must understand how the ancient Israelites lived and what they believed.

Interview the Habiru People

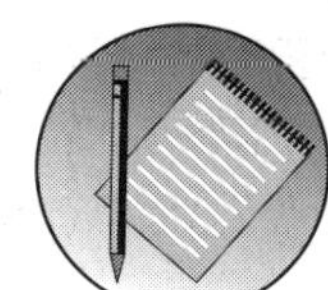

Appoint reporters to prepare questions for both groups of people: the Habiru living during good times, and the Habiru living during times of drought. In front of the class and wearing their press passes, let the reporters question various Habiru people about their lives. Let those in the audience write reports detailing the lives of these groups of people. Appoint a group of editors to take the written reports and produce a class report about the Habiru people for inclusion in the *Ancient Israelite Times*.

Write First-Person Narratives

Encourage students to revisit *Map of Ancient Israel* (page 3). Let them find the Kingdom of Israel. Have the students imagine that they are back in the time before the kingdom of Israel came into being. Migratory groups of nomads called the Habiru are trying to survive by herding. By looking at the map, have students brainstorm what the climate must have been like for these shepherds. Have students imagine the good times, back in those days, when the Habiru's herds and flocks of animals had good grazing land and the Habiru lived in relative comfort. Then have students predict what would happen to the Habiru in times of drought. Students should realize that during these terrible times, the nomads would have to leave their grazing lands in hopes of finding a more suitable place to live. Struggles would break out regarding who should have the best grazing land.

Divide the class in half, and have half the students write short first-person narratives about being a nomad in ancient Israel when life was good. Have the other students write about being a nomad during a time of drought. Let them produce first-hand accounts of the prosperous times and the miseries suffered because of the lack of water. Encourage students to share what they have written.

Laws and Beliefs

During some of the time the Habiru people were living in Canaan, or ancient Israel, Mesopotamia was ruled by Hammurabi, who reigned from 1792 to 1750 B.C. Hammurabi's Code, or set of laws, greatly influenced the development of Near Eastern civilization for centuries after it was written.

Also, during this time, the vast majority of people living in the area were *polytheistic*, believing in many gods.

Hammurabi's Code

Comparing Uses of the Torah

Discuss with students that the first five books of the Bible's Old Testament, called the Torah by the Jewish people, record the main body of history of the ancient Israelites. Explain that corroborating evidence has been found for some events in the Torah by archaeologists and historians. Other events described in the Torah have no other evidence to support them. Part of this is because the Torah was written not only as history, but as a statement of belief by the ancient Israelites of faith in their God.

Give each student a copy of *The Torah* (page 10), and have them fill it out. Then ask for two volunteers. One volunteer can pretend to be a historian or archaeologist and explain how the Torah can be used as a tool for understanding history. The other volunteer may pretend to be an ancient Israelite and explain how the Torah gives insight into the nature of one god.

Recreate Hammurabi's Code

Have students work in groups to investigate the Code of Hammurabi. A stela bearing the code was discovered in Sus, Iran, in 1901. The code was made up of 282 provisions grouped under several subheadings. The code contained important principles, such as the strong should not injure the weak and that the punishment should fit the crime. Punishments were severe, however, such as "an eye for an eye and a tooth for a tooth."

After students have learned about the Code of Hammurabi, give each group a copy of *Writing Hammurabi's Code* (page 8). Assign each group a type of law such as family, real estate, business, or labor. Let each group make up four laws in their subject area, give the rationale for each law, and tell the penalty that must be paid for breaking the law. Then have the groups share their laws with each other as a class.

Research Polytheism and Monotheism

Have the students work as partners. Let one partner study polytheism while the other partner studies monotheism. Allow the partners to exchange information about what they have learned. Then give each group of partners a copy of *Monotheism and Polytheism* (page 9), and have the partners complete the chart and answer the questions.

Writing Hammurabi's Code

Name ______________________

Here's a chance to help King Hammurabi write his code of laws. Decide on the type of law you are interested in, and circle it from the choices below. Then, list four laws that you have decided on. Give the rationale for each law and the penalty imposed if the law is broken.

Engraved on a seven-foot-high monument of black dorite, King Hammurabi of Babylon compiled 282 laws around 1800 B.C. that held citizens accountable for their actions.

family laws	laws about personal property	business laws
labor laws		real estate laws

Law 1

____

____

Rationale

____

____

____

Penalty for Breaking the Law

____

____

Law 3

____

____

Rationale

____

____

____

Penalty for Breaking the Law

____

____

Law 2

____

____

Rationale

____

____

____

Penalty for Breaking the Law

____

____

Law 4

____

____

Rationale

____

____

____

Penalty for Breaking the Law

____

____

Monotheism and Polytheism

Name ______________________________

At the time of Abraham, people in Mesopotamia worshiped thousands of gods. People in Egypt worshiped many nature gods. The ancient Israelites introduced a new idea. They worshiped only one god.

Put a check in the appropriate column in the chart to compare monotheism and polytheism.

	Monotheism	Polytheism
Which belief is probably easier to understand?		
Which belief encourages various people to choose which deity to worship?		
Which belief would encourage the development of cults dedicated to a particular god?		
Which belief would probably tend to unite people who support it?		
For most people, which belief has survived into modern times?		

From your research, explain briefly why you believe monotheism is more popular than polytheism in our times.

____

____

____

____

____

____

The Torah

Name ______________________

Which facts about the Torah, or first five books of the Old Testament, support the use of the Torah as a historical document, and which facts support its use as a religious document? Put a check in the appropriate column.

	Torah as a Historical Document	Torah as a Religious Document
Archaeologists have uncovered Hammurabi's Code, which is mentioned in the Torah.		
The ancient Israelites wrote their stories in the Torah to express their faith in God.		
Historians have found that some of the information in the Torah is supported by other historical evidence.		
The stories in the Torah tell how the god of the Israelites is powerful over history and nature.		

Explain briefly how you think historians separate what they feel is factual in the Torah from what is religious.

____

____

____

What kind of stories do you think appear in the Torah that historians may debate whether they are historical or religious?

____

____

____

Why do you think it is sometimes difficult to read the Torah as a historical source?

____

____

____

Abraham

One of the most interesting aspects of the ancient Israelites is the study of their *patriarchs*, or the founders of their faith. Abraham, Isaac, and Jacob are the patriarchs of the ancient Israelites. Their stories, which are found in the Torah, provide a rich source for the literature, tradition, and belief of the Hebrew people.

The Torah tells us that Patriarch Abraham is the first ancient Israelite to be called a Hebrew. One night Abraham prayed to the stars in the night sky. During his prayers, he had a life-changing revelation—the Lord appeared to Abraham.

Abraham knew then that there was one God. God told Abraham, "Get thee out of thy country, and from thy father's house, unto the land that I will show thee. And I will make of thee a great nation, and I will bless thee, and make thy name great."

Abraham did as the Lord said, but when he reached Canaan, the land that the Lord had promised him, he found a great famine. Because of this, Abraham and his wife Sarah migrated to Egypt, where Abraham prospered. But prosperity did not bring contentment. Abraham longed for the land of Canaan which the Lord had promised him.

Talk About the Story

Invite students to discuss why this story from the Torah would interest the ancient Israelites. How could the ancient Israelites relate the story's setting to their own lives? (Like Abraham, the ancient Israelites were wanderers, always in search of better land.) Would the ancient Israelites see Abraham as a hero? Why or why not? (The ancient Israelites probably would see Abraham as a hero, because he listens to God and does the best he can.)

Abraham and his followers traveling to Egypt

Isaac

For years Abraham and Sarah had no children, although they both wanted children desperately. Finally, Sarah gave birth to a baby boy, Isaac. Abraham and Sarah were filled with joy.

One day the Lord appeared again to Abraham. The Lord said, "Take now thy son, thine only son, whom thou lovest, and get thee unto the land of Moriah; and offer him there for a burnt-offering upon the mountain."

Abraham was heartsick, but he obeyed the Lord. Abraham carefully built a sacrificial altar on Mount Moriah, loaded it with wood, and laid Isaac on the wood. At the last moment before Isaac was to be killed, the Lord intervened and saved Isaac, saying, ". . . now I know that you are a God-fearing man."

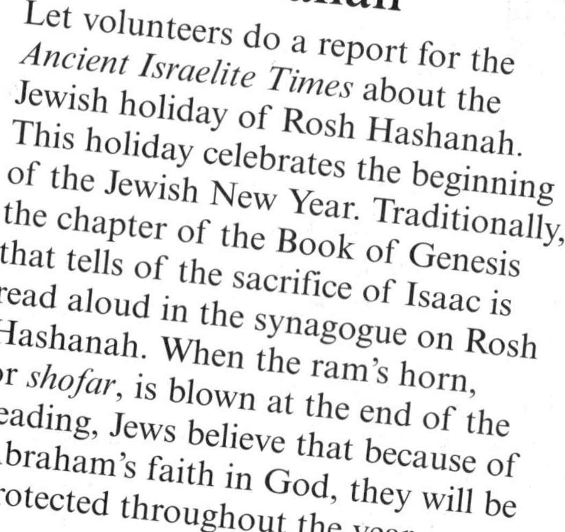

Find Out About Rosh Hashanah

Let volunteers do a report for the *Ancient Israelite Times* about the Jewish holiday of Rosh Hashanah. This holiday celebrates the beginning of the Jewish New Year. Traditionally, the chapter of the Book of Genesis that tells of the sacrifice of Isaac is read aloud in the synagogue on Rosh Hashanah. When the ram's horn, or *shofar*, is blown at the end of the reading, Jews believe that because of Abraham's faith in God, they will be protected throughout the year.

As the report is being given, you may want to serve some apple dipped in honey, a traditional dish celebrating the sweetness of the upcoming year.

Abraham and Isaac

Weigh Abraham's Decision

In small groups, have students list options Abraham could have taken regarding the sacrificing of Isaac. For example, Abraham could have ignored God's command, he could have questioned it, he could have pleaded with God, or he could (as he did) follow God's command. Encourage students to explore what might have happened if Abraham had made a different decision. Have students discuss whether Abraham's decision was the best one. Then have a spokesperson for each group report that group's discussion to the class.

Jacob

Jacob is the third of the patriarchs. This is his story.

After many years, Isaac and his wife Rebekah had twin boys. They were named Esau and Jacob. Esau, his father's favorite, was fierce and warlike. Jacob, his mother's favorite, was meek and gentle.

As Isaac grew older and lay dying, he became blind. He called for Esau so that he could confer a blessing on him. Rebekah overheard the request and told Jacob that he should receive the blessing instead. Jacob reluctantly obeyed. When Esau heard about the blessing, he was furious and vowed to kill Jacob.

Jacob fled from his house toward the town of Haran. That night, on his journey, he had a dream. In the dream, God spoke to Jacob. "I am the Lord," He said, "the God of Abraham and the God of Isaac. I give to you and your people the land whereon you lie. Your people shall be as the dust of the earth and your people shall spread abroad to the west, to the east, to the north and to the south. And all your people shall be blessed. I am with you wherever you go and I will bring you back to this land."

Jacob stayed away for many years, but one day he spotted Esau headed toward him with an armed band of men. The night before they were to meet, Jacob went off by himself to meditate.

It was then that Jacob spent the night wrestling with an angel. The angel blessed Jacob and said, "Your name shall be called no more Jacob, but Israel; for you have striven with God and with man and have prevailed."

When Jacob and Esau met, there was no bitterness. They wept in each others arms and were reconciled.

Construct a Family Tree

Give each student a copy of *Family Tree* (page 14) and have them recall the events in the story to fill out the information about the patriarchs. Then have students fill in similar information about their family. Encourage students to compare and contrast dramatic events in the lives of the patriarchs with dramatic events in their own family.

The meeting of Jacob and Esau

Make a Story Map

Let students work in pairs to complete the *Patriarchs' Story Map* (page 15). When the maps are completed, encourage students to compare and contrast their maps. When a consensus has been reached about the story map that tells the clearest story about the patriarchs, ask for volunteers to copy the story map on a bulletin board entitled "The Story of the Ancient Patriarchs."

Family Tree

Name ____________________

Fill in the missing names for the family of Abraham.

Abraham married ________________ and had a son named ________________.
Isaac married ________________ and had two sons named ________________
and ________________.

Make a family tree of Abraham's family.

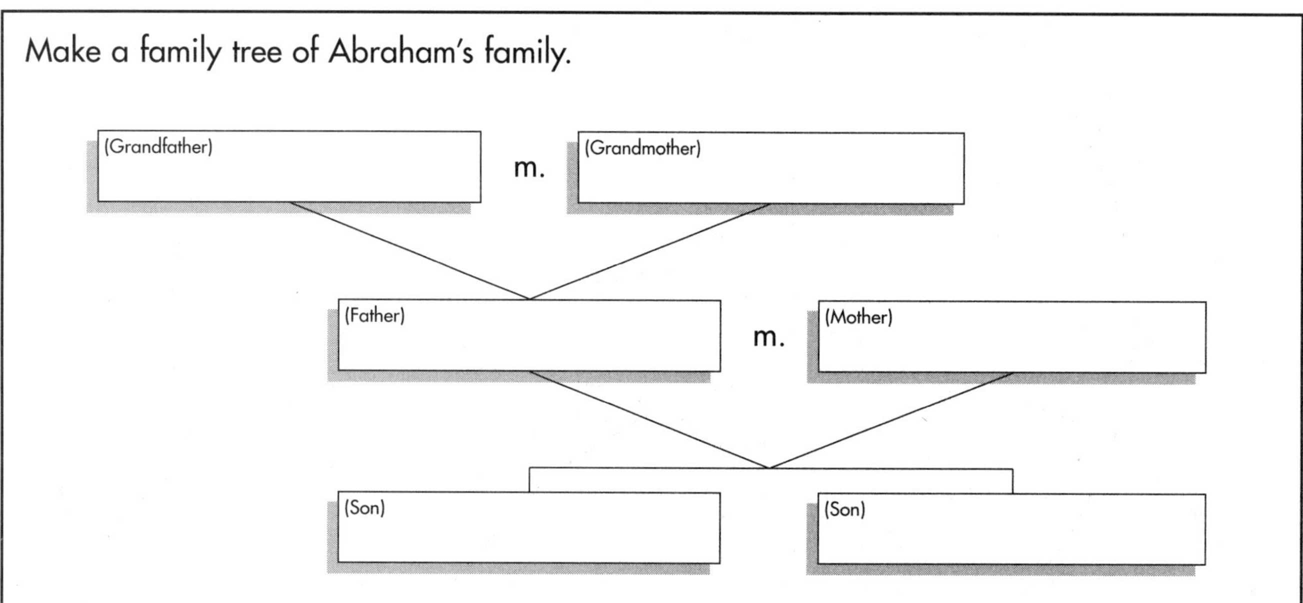

Now make a family tree with a branch of your own family.

(Grandfather) m. (Grandmother)

(Father) m. (Mother)

(Sons and Daughters) (Sons and Daughters) (Sons and Daughters) (Sons and Daughters)

Patriarchs' Story Map

Name ____________________________________

Use words and phrases to complete the story map about the patriarchs of the ancient Israelites.

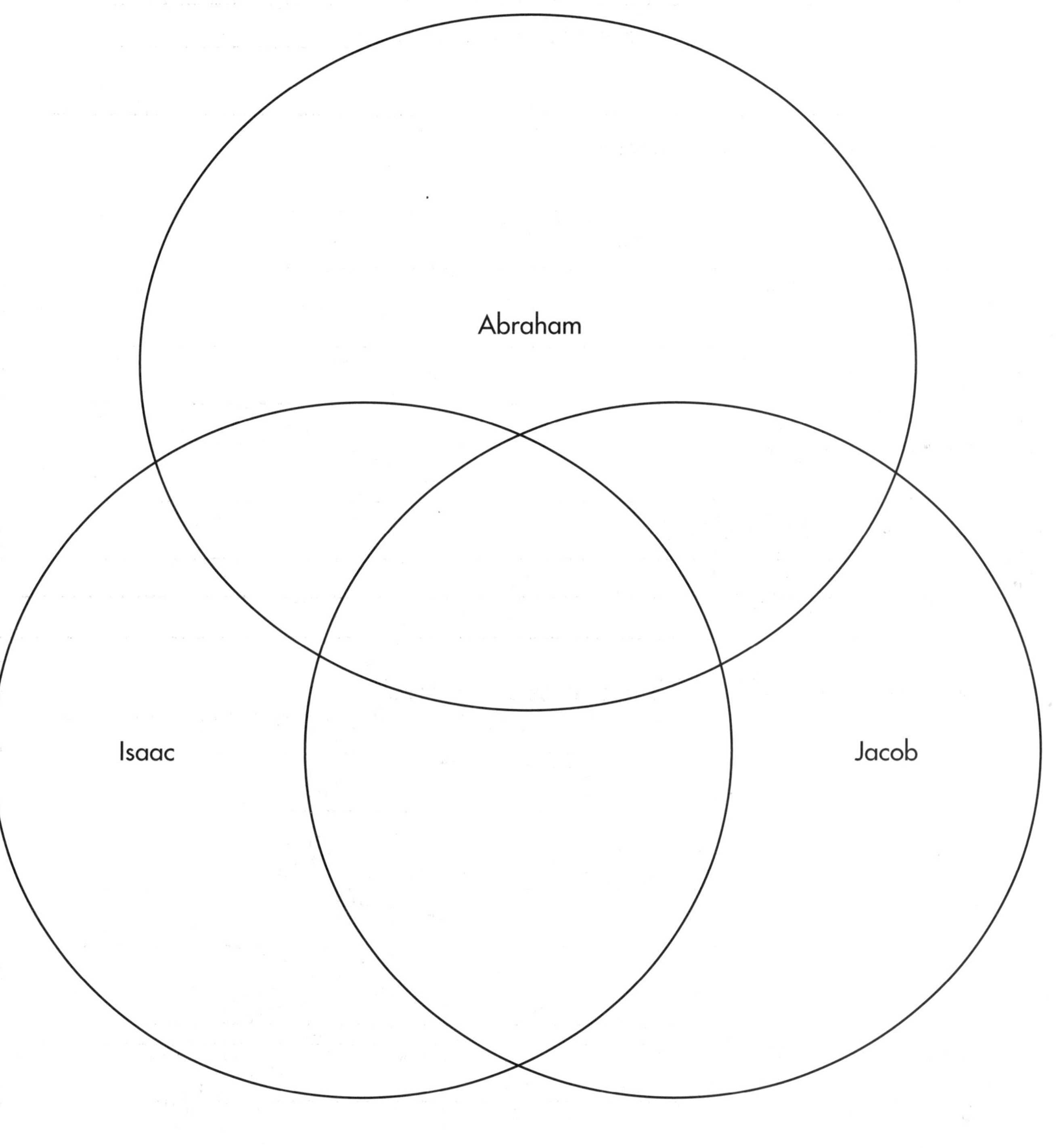

Slavery

The ancient Israelites living in Egypt grew in number until their population became quite large. This upset the pharaoh, probably Seti I, who became afraid that the Israelites would become powerful enough to upset his rule. To prevent this, he made the Israelites slaves.

After more than four hundred years of slavery, in the early 1200s B.C., Moses was born. Although an Israelite, Moses was raised in the pharaoh's household. This pharaoh was probably Ramses II. According to the Torah, God asked Moses to implore Pharaoh to let the Israelites leave Egypt. Pharaoh refused. God gave Moses miraculous powers including the ability to cause outbreaks of disease and destruction called *plagues*. Each time a plague hit, Pharaoh promised to let the Israelites go, but each time he later changed his mind.

Finally, according to the Torah, a plague came in which the first-born child of all the Egyptians died—even Pharaoh's son. After this terrible plague, Pharaoh finally let the Israelites leave Egypt.

Slaves making bricks

Write a Persuasive Letter

Have students research what life was like for the ancient Israelites under Egyptian rule. Tell students to imagine that they are Israelite slaves who can write. Have them compose a persuasive letter to Pharaoh to tell why the Israelites should be freed from bondage.

After several students have read their letters to the class, discuss reasons why Pharaoh might have decided to keep the slaves in bondage regardless of the consequences. Reasons may include the following: Israelite slaves were good workers who worked for free, or perhaps Pharaoh felt that his time was too important to listen to the concerns of slaves.

Defend an Issue

Just as Moses had to prepare good arguments to persuade Pharaoh to let the Israelites go, people today must address current issues and social concerns. Encourage students to pick a current issue or social concern and prepare a persuasive speech defending their points of view. Students may pick topics such as the environment, homelessness, the war against drugs, or other current topics.

Find Out More About Moses

The Torah contains fascinating literature about Moses' early life. Invite volunteers to retell the story of Moses in the bulrushes and Moses' aggression against an Egyptian taskmaster. Students may want to find famous paintings to show while they are retelling these stories.

The Life of Moses

Name ____________________

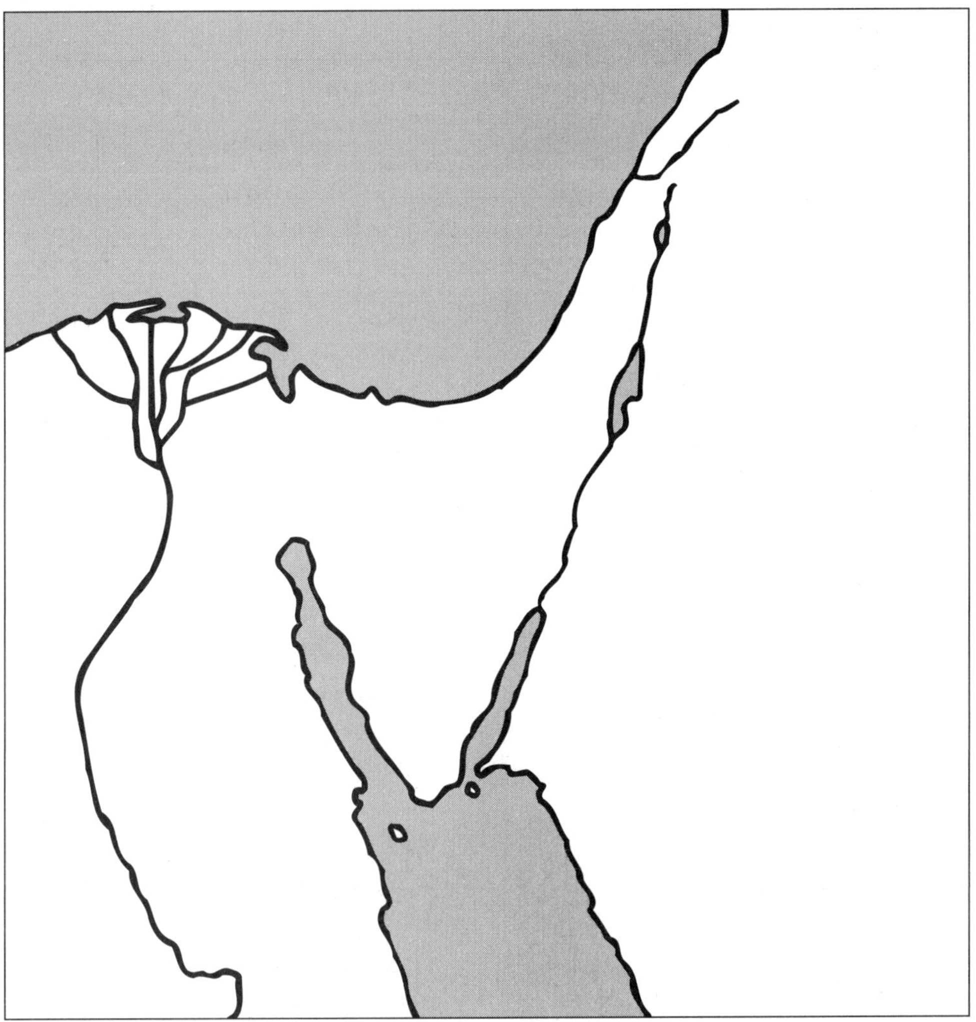

Number the map to show where the major events of Moses' life took place.

1. Moses was born a slave in Thebes, Egypt, but was raised in a royal household.

2. In Midian, Moses encountered God in a flaming bush.

3. Moses lead the Israelites out of captivity and into the wilderness known as the Sinai Peninsula.

4. Moses received the Ten Commandments from God on Mt. Sinai.

5. After forty years of wandering in the wilderness, Moses made Joshua his successor and died on Mt. Nebo, overlooking Canaan, the Promised Land.

Exodus From Egypt

Moses led the Israelites out of Egypt rejoicing. But soon they realized they were in a dangerous situation. They had to find food and water in order to survive. And the former slaves had to find a way to avoid clashes with the powerful Philistines. Moses wisely decided not to go to Canaan directly, thus avoiding the Philistines. Instead, he lead the Israelites to Canaan by a roundabout path in the wilderness. The journey was to last forty years before the Israelites reached the Promised Land.

Meanwhile, Pharaoh had second thoughts about letting the Israelites go. Pharaoh's army overtook the Israelites at the Red Sea. The Israelites were filled with panic. According to the Torah, the Lord caused the Red Sea to part so that the Israelites could escape.

Moses breaking the tablet of the law.

Snap a News Shot

Divide students into groups of five or six. Tell the students that as photojournalists they will try to recapture the events happening to the ancient Israelites. Let students pick a story, such as the ancient Israelites in slavery, Moses pleading with Pharaoh, the plagues of Egypt, the escape of the Israelites, or the parting of the Red Sea.

Have students decide how to produce props and costumes to photograph the shot that they want. Then, have them designate a photojournalist to use a camera to take the snapshot of the event. Display the snapshots on a bulletin board entitled "Slavery and Freedom."

After the photos have appeared on the bulletin board, they can be saved to be put in the *Ancient Israelite Times*.

Interview a Former Israelite Slave

Ask a volunteer to pose as an ancient Israelite who has escaped from Egypt after the Red Sea has just parted.

Have the other students wear their press passes as they question the ancient Israelite about what life was like under the pharaohs and what it is like to wander in the wilderness and to escape by the parting of the Red Sea.

Have the students write articles for their newspapers based on the interview.

Eat Passover Treats

The holiday of Passover, or *Pesah*, celebrates the freedom of the Israelites as they escape from slavery to freedom. Traditionally, the Jewish people celebrate Passover with a meal called *Seder*. The Seder meal tells the story of Passover. The following traditional foods are eaten at Seder:

- Unleavened matza bread reminds Jewish people that their ancestors had to leave Egypt so quickly that there was no time for the bread to rise.
- A roasted egg represents hope and renewal.
- A lamb bone stands for the lambs that priests sacrificed long ago in Jerusalem.
- Charoset, a mixture of apples, honey, nuts, wine, and spices represents the mortar that bound the bricks that the enslaved Israelites made for the Egyptians.
- Bitter herbs such a horseradish represent the bitterness of slavery.
- Green vegetables dipped in salt water represent the tears shed during the captivity of the Israelites.
- Wine symbolizes the promises God gave to the ancient Israelites.

Invite students to bring in as many of these foods as possible for a snack. While students are eating, review the significance of each food to the Jewish people. Have students write an article about the meal for the *Ancient Israelite Times*.

Hear the Music

Provide recordings of spirituals about the ancient Israelites. Have students tell about what is happening to the ancient Israelites in songs such as "Go Down, Moses," "Let My People Go," and "Poor Wayfaring Stranger." Let students discuss ways in which music increases understanding of historical events.

Moses

During the time the ancient Hebrews wandered through the wilderness, they lived by a set of laws. The most significant of these developed while the ancient Israelites were living near Mount Sinai. The Torah explains that about three months after the ancient Israelites left Egypt, God gave Moses laws that are known as the Ten Commandments.

The Israelites believed that if they obeyed the Ten Commandments and other laws, they would receive God's blessing and protection. This agreement is called a *covenant*.

The covenant with God associated with the Ten Commandments, in addition to being important to the Israelites, also in later centuries became a basis for both the religions of Judaism and Christianity. The Ten Commandments also give Western cultures a basis of ideas about justice and law.

The Ten Commandments

I am the Lord your God who brought you out of the land of Egypt, the house of bondage. You shall have no other gods besides me.

You shall not make for yourself a sculpted image of anything that is in heaven above.

You shall not swear falsely by the name of the Lord your God.

Remember the sabbath day and keep it holy.

Honor your father and mother.

You shall not murder.

You shall not commit adultery.

You shall not steal.

You shall not bear false witness against your neighbor.

You shall not desire anything that is your neighbor's.

Exodus 20: 3-14

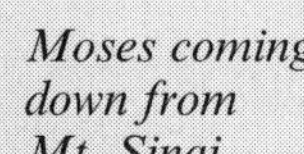

Moses coming down from Mt. Sinai

Compare the Ten Commandments With the Code of Hammurabi

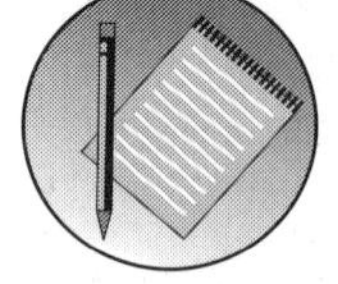

Divide the students into small groups. Let each group appoint a discussion leader and a reporter to take notes. Give each group two copies of *Compare Laws* (page 22)—one for the discussion leader and one for the reporter. Let the discussion leader read the discussion topics. After each topic has been discussed, let the reporter record the group's answers on the answer sheet.

The reporters can then post the comments their group made on the bulletin board for members of the class to read.

Interview Moses

Tell students that a great burst of flame has come from Mount Sinai. The mountain has been rumbling and smoking. When a blast or a ram's horn, or shofar was heard, Moses climbed the mountain to meet with God.

Have the students act as reporters, brainstorming questions to ask Moses when he returns to the people. After discussing several questions the reporters might ask, as well as the answers Moses might give, have several volunteers, one at a time, act as Moses and answer the reporters' questions. Have the reporters write the event as an article for the *Ancient Israelite Times*.

Moses before the burning bush

Investigate Other Aspects of Moses' Life

Encourage groups to find out and report on the worship of the golden calf and the death of Moses right before his people reached the Promised Land. Challenge the groups to find dramatic ways to portray these stories.

Compare the Ten Commandments With Current Law

Invite a lawyer to visit the class to compare and contrast current U.S. law with the Ten Commandments. Which Commandments have corresponding laws today? Which do not? Encourage discussions about why some Commandments have carried over legally into our time and why some have not.

Develop Ten Commandments for Your School

After studying the Ten Commandments, give each student a copy of *Ten School Commandments* (page 23). Invite students to think about ten rules that all members of your school could follow to make the school a better place.

When the students have finished writing their own set of ten rules, compare the rules and come up with a consensus for ten commandments for your school.

Have students discuss how the school as a whole would get along better if everyone believed and followed these ten rules. Have students explain how the Ten Commandments may have unified the ancient Israelites.

Compare Laws

Name ______________________

As a group, discuss the following questions. Appoint one member of your group as a recorder and have that person write down the group's answers in the spaces provided.

1. There are ten commandments, but Hammarabi's Code has 282 laws. Which set of rules is more specific?

   ____

2. Is it better to have a long list of very specific rules or a short list of memorable rules to live by?

   ____

   Why?____

   ____

   ____

3. The Code of Hammurabi was based on earlier collections of Sumerian and Akkadian laws. The Torah says that the Ten Commandments was written by God on two stone tables and was carried to the people by Moses. Which set of laws do you think are more important to follow? Why? ______________________________

   ____

   ____

   ____

4. Why do you suppose that many people are familiar with the Ten Commandments, but not with the Code of Hammurabi? ____________________________

   ____

   ____

   ____

   ____

   ____

   ____

Ten School Commandments

Name ____________________

Write ten rules for your school that you think will make the school a better place for all students. Then, compare your rules with the rules your classmates wrote.

Ten Commandments for ____________________ School

1.

2.

3.

4.

5.

6.

7.

8.

9.

10.

The Ark of the Covenant

The ark of the covenant was the object most sacred to the Israelites as they traveled through the wilderness. Inside the ark, or covenant box, were the two stone tablets containing the Ten Commandments that Moses received from God at Mount Sinai. The ark also contained a golden jar of manna, which was a reminder of God's provision for his people in exile.

Archaeologists and historians are reasonably sure what the ark looked like, because there is a description of it in Exodus 25:10-22, and a stone carving of the ark was found at the excavation of a synagogue in Capernaum.

The ark was a box about 45 inches long, 27 inches wide, and 27 inches high. It was made of acacia wood. The lid was made of gold. Mounted on the lid were two creatures with wings. The figures faced each other, and their wings were unfurled. The Israelites believed that God lived among them between the wings of the cherubim.

Investigate Manna

The ark of the covenant contained a golden jar of manna to help the Israelites remember that manna was the food miraculously given by God to the Israelites during their wandering in the wilderness. Have students act as investigative reporters to find out what the manna may have really been. First, have various reporters find instances of manna mentioned in the Bible. They should find references in the following places: Exodus 16:4, Deuteronomy 8:16, Exodus 16:16-18, Exodus 16:31, Exodus 17:6, Exodus 16:13.

Then have other reporters find out what manna may have been made of. (Some historians believe that manna was a substance secreted by plant parasites as they fed on tamarisk trees in the wilderness.)

Draw the Ark of the Covenant

Let students research how cherubim or wing angels look in various paintings. Then invite students to draw their own version of how the lid to the ark of covenant might have looked. Also encourage some students to research how the ark of the covenant was believed to have helped Joshua win the battle of Jericho. Other students can find out when and where the ark disappeared.

The Battle of Jericho

After years of wandering in the wilderness, Moses died just before leading his people into the Promised Land. Joshua was Moses' second in command. He lead the Israelites into the Promised Land.

The first obstacle was the city of Jericho. The fields around Jericho were planted with crops or had flocks grazing on them. But the city itself was formidable. Archaeologists have discovered that the city was only about six acres in size, but was surrounded by two sets of walls. The first was six feet thick, and the inner wall was twelve feet thick.

Joshua's soldiers surrounded Jericho. No one could enter or leave the city's gates. The Bible tells us that Joshua gave the signal and priests blew their shofars, or ram's horns, and the ancient Israelites shouted outside the walls. On the seventh day the noise caused the walls of Jericho to crack and crumble, and the ancient Israelites overtook the city.

The conquest of Jericho

Investigate Evidence

Archaeologists who uncovered Jericho have found that it is in an earthquake zone. In 1927, an earthquake hit the ruins of Jericho and sent cliffs crashing into the nearby Jordan river. Some archaeologists say that the walls of Jericho were tumbled by an earthquake.

Invite students to discuss what they think might have happened and how they can corroborate their evidence.

Sing the Song

Encourage students to discuss how Joshua and the other Israelites might have felt before the battle when they found out how well-fortressed Jericho was. Then have them talk about how jubilant the Israelites must have felt when they won the battle. Have students sing or listen to the song "Joshua Fought the Battle of Jericho."

The Flowering of Israel

After Joshua brought the Israelites back into the land of Canaan, or Israel, they prospered. Many Israelites ceased to be nomads and began an agricultural way of life. This enabled them to live in one place, so they built houses.

The ancient Israelites wore wool clothing if they were poor, and linen if they were well-off. The wealthy also wore cotton from Egypt and silk from India and China.

While the men worked as shepherds or farmers, the women did most of the household work including grinding grain, baking bread, pressing olives, and making cheese and butter. Women carded the wool for the family, combed the yarn, spindled the thread, wove the cloth, and sewed the garments. Women also helped gather the harvest.

Investigate Ancient Fabrics

Divide the class into four groups, and have each group investigate one of the fabrics used in the ancient world: wool, linen, cotton, and silk. Let each group find out where the fabric they are investigating comes from and the process it goes through before it can be used as fabric.

Have each group write a fashion article for the *Ancient Israelite Times* telling about the fabric, its properties, and the kinds of clothes the ancient Israelites might have used it for. When the articles are completed and edited, make copies of all the articles to distribute to each student so that he or she can include them in his or her edition of the *Ancient Israelite Times*.

Ruth in the field of Boaz

Discuss Roles

Hold a class discussion about why in ancient Israel, the men had the role of shepherd or farmer while the women did work around the house. Ask the students to name some social changes that have made the social structure of our society different than that of the ancient Israelites.

In the course of the discussion, students may mention that in ancient Israel women had the children and needed to be around to feed the babies, and it was most practical for them to stay around the house where the children stayed. In today's society, we have enough automated machinery to do much of the housework, and babies and young children can be cared for by other caregivers, allowing women the opportunity to do other kinds of work.

The Land of Canaan

The older name for the land of Israel is Canaan. Canaan is also the name for the then-popular purple dye made from the shells of a mollusk or shellfish called the *murex*. The dyers wore gloves to protect their hands. They mixed their dye in a stone or pottery vat, then soaked the wool cloth in the dye.

The cities in Canaan were generally built on hills. A wall was built around the cities for protection. Cities often had towers on the walls so that people could be on the lookout for an enemy attack. There was always a tower at the gate to a city. The gate to a city wasn't straight, but turned at an angle so that if enemy troops fired their arrows into the city, they wouldn't hit the soldiers.

The Hebrews lived in four-room houses. They were sometimes built in a row as a barrier against enemies.

Store Water

Tell students that although the cities were well fortified, they often did not have running water because the streams occurred naturally at the foot of the hills, rather than on the top.

Let students brainstorm ways of getting water in the midst of a siege. After the discussion, you can explain how most cities had cisterns to store extra water. Some cities even dug tunnels through the hill on which their city stood to divert water into a man-made well in the city.

Experiment With Dye

Divide students into groups of five or six. Tell each group that they are going to become dye-makers and that to produce their dyes, they need to use materials in their natural surroundings. Let students use their dyes to dye a piece of cloth that you provide. Students may try materials such as grass, beets, or grapes to produce their dyes. After each group has dyed its cloth, have each of the groups explain how they produced their dye and on what objects they might want to use the dye.

Food

Because they were farmers and shepherds, the ancient Israelites had many foods available to them including wheat, barley, lentils, grapes, olives, nuts, and milk for cheese and butter.

The ancient Israelites had a close relationship with animals and developed a very strict code detailing what animals could be eaten. They set high standards for cleanliness and humane treatment in meat preparation.

According to their dietary law, all meat, fish, and poultry eaten needed to be *kosher.* This means that when eating a meal, no meat or meat products could be cooked or eaten with any milk or dairy products. However, some foods were called *parve.* This meant they could be eaten with either meat or dairy products. Parve foods included eggs; fish with backbones, fins, and scales; vegetables; vegetable oil; fruits; bread; and pastries.

Even today, many Jewish people still follow the kosher dietary tradition.

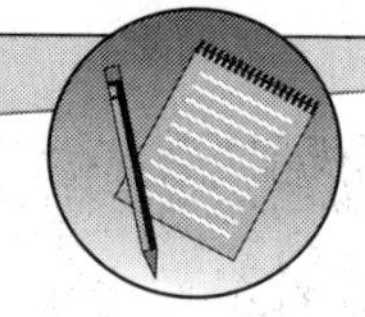

Plan a Feast

Tell the students that as reporters they will investigate the kitchens in many households before an upcoming feast. Give each student a copy of *Plan a Feast* (page 29) and tell them that the list of foods shows all that is available for the feast. As reporters, they are to report possible menus that may be used for the feast. You may want to review the basic food groups with students to make sure that they suggest balanced menus.

Answers:
Here are some possible menus.

Meat
lamb
bread and honey
cucumber and onion salad
olives
grape juice

Dairy
fish
bread and butter
cheese
olives and apples
milk

Non-Kosher items
~~cheeseburger~~
steak
~~taco~~
~~spaghetti with meatballs and Parmesan cheese~~
turkey
tossed salad
~~creamed chicken on toast~~
fruit and cheese

Discuss the Effects of a Special Diet

Ask students to tell how they think eating a special diet would affect the ancient Israelites socially. For example, would the ancient Israelites be likely to join pagan neighbors at a meal or banquet? (Chances are, the ancient Israelites would not eat with pagans, since there was no way to tell whether much of the food was kosher.) Would their common dietary restrictions tighten the bonds of community among the ancient Israelites? (Chances are they would because they all share the same dietary beliefs.)

Plan a Feast

Name ______________________

Here is a list of the foods you have found in the ancient Israelites' homes. Use the foods to create two possible kosher menus—one meat menu and one dairy menu. Remember to "keep kosher." Don't mix meat and dairy.

bread	butter	onions	cheese
olives	lamb	eggs	lettuce
apple	fish	chicken	grape juice
honey	cucumber	milk	

Feast With Meat

Feast With Dairy

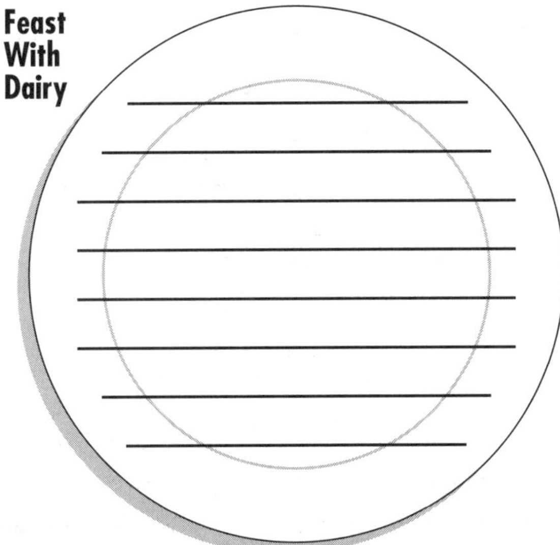

Cross out the non-kosher items from foods we eat today:

- cheeseburger
- steak
- taco
- spaghetti with meatballs and Parmesan cheese
- turkey
- tossed salad
- creamed chicken on toast
- fruit and cheese

Music and Song

Musicians and poets were important to the ancient Israelites. The Israelites' temple, or place of worship, was filled with poems to God which were set to music. These song-poems were called psalms. Even today, the psalms rank among some of the world's greatest poetry.

About half of the poems in the Old Testament of the Bible are attributed to David, the king, poet, and harpist.

Write a Song

Read one of the psalms to students. You may choose one such as the 24th Psalm:

The earth is the Lord's, and its fullness thereof; the world, and those who dwell in it. For he founded it upon the seas, and established it upon the rivers.

Encourage students to write their own song praising something they like about the world. Let students share their songs in small groups and set the ones they like best to music. Then let each group prepare a song for presentation to the class, using the timbrels to keep the rhythm.

Make a Timbrel

In ancient Israel, people loved to sing and dance. One of the instruments used by singers to accompany themselves was the timbrel. This instrument was like a tambourine.

Let your students make a timbrel. Each student needs an aluminum pie pan, some dried beans, a piece of plastic wrap large enough to cover the pie pan, and some cellophane mailing tape.

1. Have students put several beans in the aluminum pie pan.
2. Cover the pie pan with the plastic wrap.
3. Use the tape to tape the plastic wrap tightly around the pie plate.
4. Tell students that in ancient Israel, people sang and danced to music that had a strong beat. Let students practice singing songs they know and keeping rhythm to them by beating the aluminum pie plate side of their timbrels.

The Hebrew Language

The ancient Israelites spoke Hebrew. The Torah and other religious books were written in Hebrew. Hebrew's written form evolved from the Phoenician alphabet.

Hebrew is read from right to left, and Hebrew books open from left to right. The Hebrew language does not use capital letters.

Haggadhah page showing the service of Passover

Learn the Hebrew Alphabet

Give each student a copy of *The Hebrew Alphabet* (page 34), and let your class do the following activities:

- Have the students study all the Hebrew letters. Then challenge the students to see how many letters they can write from memory.
- Have students practice saying the letters in the Hebrew alphabet aloud as they look at them. Write various letters on the board, and have students identify them.
- Have each student write his or her name. Below the name, have the student write his or her name in Hebrew letters, starting at the right, and working toward the left. Tell students to use the letters that are closest to the English sounds.

Make a Hebrew Language Bulletin Board

Display common objects or put pictures of common objects on the bulletin board. Under each object, write the object's name in Hebrew, its pronunciation, and the name in English. Here are some examples:

גַּרְבַּיִם
(gar-BAH-yim)
socks

חָתוּל
(chah-TOOL)
cat

עֲנָק
(ah-NAHK)
giant

דָּגִים
(dah-GEEM)
fish

בָּרָק
(bah-RAHK)
lightning

לְבָנָה
(leh-vah-NAH)
moon

הוֹרִים
(hoh-REEM)
parents

יָד
(yahd)
hand

פַּרְפָּרִים
(pahr-pah-REEM)
butterflies

Ancient Games

Just as children do today, the children of the ancient Israelites enjoyed playing games.

One popular game played during the Jewish celebration of Chanukah is dreidel. The dreidel is a top. In Yiddish, its name means *turn*.

There are four letters on the dreidel, one on each side:

ג	=	Gimmel
נ	=	Nun
ה	=	Heh
ש	=	Shin

They stand for the words *Nes Gadel Hayah Sham*, which means "A Great Miracle Happened There."

Make a Dreidel

Divide students into groups of four or five. Give each group a floral block, a 1/2" dowel, (These can be purchased in a craft shop.) thumb tacks, scissors, construction paper, a marker, and a blunt-tipped knife.

Draw a picture of a dreidel on the board and have students work together to problem-solve making a dreidel from the materials at hand.

Students should come to the conclusion they they need to use the knife to cut the floral block so that it has a pointed bottom, insert the dowel rod into the top of the dreidel, write the letters using the markers, trim the construction paper, and tack the letters to the sides of the dreidel.

Play Dreidel

Allow each group to play dreidel. Give everyone an equal number of markers. Each player should put one marker in the middle. The first player spins the dreidel.

If it lands on Nun, the player does nothing.

If it lands on Gimmel, the player takes everything in the middle.

If it lands on Hey, the player takes half the markers.

If it lands on Shin, the player puts one in.

An easy way to remember the rules is

N = Nothing

G = Get

H = Half

SH = Share

Everyone puts another marker in the middle before the next player spins the dreidel.

You can also make a Dreidel using a pencil and some construction paper.

Get the Scoop on Sports

When various groups are playing dreidel by using the markers and/or adding numbers, appoint a few "roving sportscasters" to report on the "scores" after the activities are finished.

Hunt the Dreidel

As a whole class activity, have one person leave the room while another person hides the dreidel. When the student returns to the room to find the dreidel, have the rest of the students sing a work song they made up for the exercise on page 40. Let the students sing louder when the seeker gets closer to the dreidel and sing softer when the seeker moves away from the dreidel.

Vary the Game

Hebrew letters also stand for numbers.

Nun = 50
Gimmel = 3
Hey = 5
Shin = 300

Have the students take turns in their groups spinning the dreidel. After each spin, have someone record each player's score. The first person who scores 1,000 wins.

The Hebrew Alphabet

Name ____________________

Study the Hebrew letters below. Then, write your name in the box provided. Below your name, write it again using Hebrew letters.

Hebrew Letter	Letter Name	Equivalent Sound
א	ALEF	takes the sound of its accompanying vowel
בּ	BET	B as in Book
ג	GIMMEL	G as in Good
ד	DALET	D as in Dance
ה	HEY	H as in Hop
ו	VAV	V as in Very
ז	ZAYIN	Z as in Zoo
ח	HET	CH as in Chirp
ט	TET	T as in Top
י	YOD	Y as in Yes
כּ	KAF	K as in Kind
ל	LAMED	L as in Light
מ	MEM	M as in Make
נ	NUN	N as in Note
ס	SAMEKH	S as in Same
ע	AYIN	takes the sound of its accompanying vowel
פּ	PAY	P as in Pass
צ	TZADEEK	TZ as in tzar
ק	KOF	K as in Kind
ר	RESH	R as in Rock
שׁ	SHIN	SH as in Shell
ת	TAV	T as in Tell

Storytelling

There was little paper or papyrus in ancient Israel. People wrote on clay or on limestone tablets which was a cumbersome process. Because of this, much of the ancient Israelites' tradition and history was passed down orally. It became very important to them to be able to memorize and tell the story of their people.

Tell a Story

Ask for volunteer storytellers to pretend to be ancient Israelites. Have them tell the class a story about something that happened to the ancient Israelites. Encourage students to be as dramatic as possible in their storytelling. Allow them to use props if they choose to.

Retell a Story

Divide students into groups of five or six. Have one person in the group silently read a short account about something that happened to the ancient Israelites and whisper it to another member of the group. Let that student whisper it to the next, and so on. Have the last person retell the story as he or she heard it. Have them discuss differences in the story the last person heard from the printed version. Let them speculate about why this may have occurred.

It wasn't until much later that stories were written on papyrus.

Ancient Tools

People started using tools early in ancient times. The first tools were probably knives for obtaining animal meat and scrapers and hoes for tilling the soil. By the time of the ancient Israelites, builders, carpenters, farmers, fishermen, potters, householders, and metal smiths all had special tools.

Tell students that they are going to pose as craftspersons to get an idea of how the people in ancient Israel did their jobs.

Throw a Pot

The potter's wheel was an early invention. It hasn't changed much in six thousand years. Invite students posing as potters to find out and explain how the potter's wheel works. They also might want to display pots made on a potter's wheel and discuss the kinds of useful objects that can be made on a potter's wheel.

This vase shaped like a man's head was made in about 1700 B.C.

Be a Master Builder

Let the students in this group learn how a measuring line is used in building. Tell students that the unit of measure in the time of the ancient Israelites was the *cubit,* which was 17.5 inches long, or about as long as the distance from the tip of the middle finger to the elbow. Let the builders measure several things in the classroom using cubits and report their length. Also have builders investigate and demonstrate how a plumb line is used.

Demonstrate Carpentry

Many of the carpenters' tools in use today were used in ancient times. Encourage students to bring from home and demonstrate various tools such as a marking tool, a tape measure, an awl, a saw, a nail, a chisel, and a bow drill. Have students talk about how these tools are used in products now and encourage the students to speculate about the types of tools that were used in ancient times.

Farming the Land

The ancient Israelites adapted to their environment as all successful civilizations must do. Where there was soil and water, crops were planted. Where there was only grass and rocks, shepherd tended flocks of goats and sheep.

Around 925 B.C. an inscription was written on a stone tablet by an ancient boy from Gezer as a school composition. This tablet, called the Gezer Calendar, lists the seasons for planting and harvesting. According to this calendar, the olive harvest lasted two months, grain planting two months, late planting two months, and flax hoeing, the barley harvest, the wheat harvest, and the gathering of summer fruits one month each.

Grapes were also grown in ancient Israel. To make a vineyard, ancient Israelites removed stone from the fields and built walls with them. They then planted vines and trained them to grow up trees or sticks. Wine presses were also made from stones found in the fields.

Investigate the Tools of Farming

Students can investigate why the yoke and traces (leather straps) were necessary for getting oxen to help with plowing. They can also investigate the use of the plow, the axe, and the sickle. Providing pictures of these objects while they are being discussed would be helpful.

Guards kept a close watch over vineyards.

Run an Ancient Household

Have students investigate the early ovens that were usually built into courtyards. Students might also want to find out how grain was milled, and how a press was used to extract juices from grapes, olives, and other fruit. They may want to discuss the amount of work it took to keep a household in ancient Israel and the amount of time it takes for housework in present-day America.

David and Goliath

Saul, the first king of Israel, had developed a nervous condition and needed someone to calm him. It was then that David, a young shepherd in Bethlehem, was asked to play his harp for King Saul.

The year was about 1000 B.C. Israel was having a war with the Philistines, who were fighting over control of Canaan. One of the Philistines was the giant Goliath, a great warrior. Goliath taunted the Israelites as being weaklings. "Choose one of your men," he challenged, ". . . if he is able to fight with me and kill me, then we will become your slaves; but if I best him, you shall be our slaves . . . "

David the harpist decided to accept the challenge. He went to a brook, gathered five smooth stones and went to face Goliath. The first stone David slung hit Goliath in the forehead, and he fell face down on the ground. David had killed Goliath with the one stone.

When King Saul and David returned to their people, the women of the city came singing and dancing, with timbrels and with three-stringed instruments.

Compare David With Modern Heroes

Have students do research on modern-day heroes. They may be heroes currently in the news or well-known figures from our country's past. Have each student write a short paper comparing and contrasting his or her hero with David. Read the most thought-provoking papers aloud to the class.

David casting a stone at Goliath

Explore Points of View

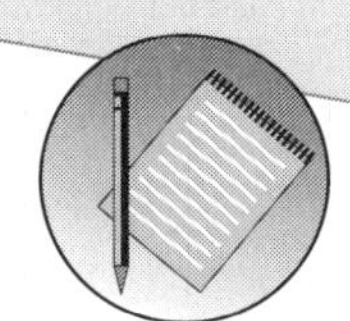

Assign half the class to be Philistine reporters covering the battle between David and Goliath. The other students can be ancient Israelite reporters covering the same story. Let each group decide the angle from which they will cover their story. Then have each reporter write his or her own story. Ask for volunteers to share their stories. Have students save their stories for the *Ancient Israelite Times*.

David, King of Israel

David ruled Israel for forty years. In doing this, he brought together all the tribes of ancient Israel for the first time. With Israel behind him as a nation, David was finally able to defeat the Philistines, who had been bitter enemies for many years.

David also captured the city of Jerusalem. He called Jerusalem "The City of David" and made it the capital of the Israelite nation. David's rule marked the beginning of a dynasty that was to last more than four hundred years.

Study the Current News

Have students study current or recent news stories to find out about a person who has recently become the leader of a country. Have a class discussion about the way in which this individual became the leader of his or her nation. Have students compare this with David's rise to power.

Create a Mural of Jerusalem

Have groups of students do research to find out what Jerusalem looked like when David was king. Have students use the information and pictures they find to create a mural of Jerusalem. The students can do preliminary sketches using pencil, then complete the picture using poster paint. After the murals are completed, have students research and explain how David was able to conquer Jerusalem.

King David rejoicing

King Solomon

After David's death, his son Solomon became king. The name Solomon means *peace* in Hebrew, and while Solomon was king, peace prevailed. Solomon was considered to be a very wise person. According to the Bible, Solomon "spoke three thousand proverbs (wise sayings) and his songs were a thousand and five."

Solomon made wise business dealings with the pharaoh of Egypt and other rulers. He also found additional countries to trade with Israel, increasing Israel's wealth.

Unfortunately, King Solomon decreed building projects that were so expensive that the Israelites were burdened with heavy taxes. People became upset, too, when King Solomon ordered the men of Israel to work on the buildings without pay.

Understand Proverbs

Ask students to think of some wise sayings they know. They may think of sayings such as "An apple a day keeps the doctor away." or "Early to bed and early to rise makes a man healthy, wealthy, and wise."

Give students a copy of *Proverbs of Solomon* (page 41). After they have written interpretations of the proverbs, encourage them to discuss what they think the proverbs mean and whether or not the students feel that the message of the proverbs is true.

Then have the students read their own proverbs. Have them recopy their proverbs on pieces of construction paper. Display them on a bulletin board entitled "Wise Words for Our Times."

King Solomon

Compose a Work Song

Let students form groups of four or five. Remind students that the ancient Israelites were great lovers of music. The harvesters sang songs in the field as they worked, and those who labored on the temple worked to the rhythm of songs. Encourage the students to imagine that they are laborers taking in a harvest or cutting or hauling stones for the temple. Have them make up appropriate work songs to go with familiar tunes, such as "I've Been Working on the Railroad," "She'll Be Comin' Round the Mountain When She Comes," and "Casey Jones." Invite the groups to perform their songs in front of the class either pantomiming the work movements of the laborers or playing their timbrels.

Proverbs of Solomon

Name ________________________

In your own words, explain what these Proverbs of Solomon mean.

1. He who walks honestly walks securely, but he whose ways are crooked will fare badly. (Proverbs 10: 9)

   Meaning: ____

   ____

2. Like choice silver is the just man's tongue; the heart of the wicked is of little worth. (Proverbs 10: 20)

   Meaning: ____

   ____

3. Poverty and shame befall the man who disregard correction, but he who heeds reproof is honored. (Proverbs 13: 18)

   Meaning: ____

   ____

4. The fool takes no delight in understanding, but rather in displaying what he thinks. (Proverbs 18: 2)

   Meaning: ____

   ____

5. Like a club, or a sword, or a sharp arrow, is the man who bears false witness against his neighbor. (Proverbs 25: 18)

   Meaning: ____

   ____

Now write a proverb of your own.

Proverb: ____

____

Meaning: ____

____

The Temple

Solomon's most popular and most magnificent building project was the main temple in Jerusalem. The temple was important to the Israelites as a center for worshiping God. It became a symbol for the Jewish faith.

The temple was not large—about 120 feet long, 40 feet wide, and 60 feet high according to the Bible—but had great beauty. Ivory covered the outer doors, gold decorated the walls of the holiest rooms, and special cedar beams from Lebanon formed the roof. The hill on which the temple was built was called Zion.

TV Coverage for Solomon's Temple

Ask for volunteers to report on the completion of the temple for a TV audience. Have each reporter show various features of the temple and interview another student acting as King Solomon. Solomon can explain the rationale for building the temple, the cost in money and labor, and its importance to the people.

King Solomon's Temple

Research the Brazen Sea

In front of the temple, Solomon built a huge bronze bowl resting on twelve bronze oxen arranged in groups of three. This was called the brazen sea. The brazen sea held about sixteen thousand gallons of water.

Have one group of students find out the purpose of the brazen sea, and draw a picture of what they think it looked like. Students should find that the brazen sea was used by temple priests to ritually wash their hands and feet before services.

Have another group research how the brazen sea was made. Students should find that bronze is an alloy of copper and tin. Archaeologists have found that a depression called *Wadi el-Arabah*, a depression running from the Dead Sea to the Red Sea, was the source of the copper. This area was known as King Solomon's mines. Encourage students to find out how the copper was mined, how it was mixed with tin, cast, and made into the brazen sea.

Interior of King Solomon's Temple

Solomon's Wisdom

Retell the story about the incident in King Solomon's reign when two women came before him, each claiming to be mother of a baby. Solomon ordered the baby be cut in half. One woman accepted Solomon's judgment. The other woman protested that the first woman could have the baby. Solomon gave the baby to the second woman because he knew that the real mother would not allow her baby to be cut in half.

Encourage students to role-play this incident and to make up other incidents that could show Solomon's wisdom.

Explore the Dome of the Rock

Have students read about and find pictures of the Dome of the Rock. Let some students find out why Moslems, Jews, and Christians all feel that this spot is sacred. Students should find that Moslems believe that souls will be judged there. Jews and Christians believe that this is the site of Solomon's Temple.

Dome of the Rock

The Wailing Wall

Find Out About The Wailing Wall

Let students research the history of The Wailing Wall in Jerusalem. Students should find out that this wall is not the remains of Solomon's Temple, but of another temple that King Herod built. You might want to invite a Jewish person into the class to explain the significance of The Wailing Wall today in Jerusalem. Pictures of modern-day Jews at the Wall give a sense of its historical importance.

A Divided Kingdom

After King Solomon died, his son Rehoboam demanded even more forced labor and taxes than his father had. The people revolted. The people in northern Israel decided to choose their own king. Rehoboam was powerless to stop them.

The northern kingdom continued to be known as Israel. Its capital was Shechem. The southern kingdom, still ruled by Rehoboam, was named Judah. Its capital was Jerusalem.

The two countries existed side by side for years, but there was much political upheaval. Eventually, the Assyrians conquered Israel in 721 B.C. In 586 B.C., the Babylonians conquered Judah.

Write to Dear Deborah

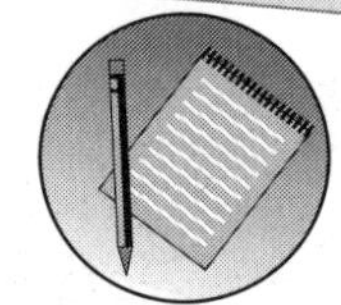

Have students pretend that there was an advice columnist in ancient Israel around the time the people were oppressed and the kingdom was divided. People wrote to her about all kinds of hardships in their lives—everything from complaints that the breadwinner in the family was forced into slave labor to worries that families had no money for food after they paid taxes.

Have each student write a letter to Dear Deborah explaining his or her problem. Then have the students exchange papers, and pretending to be Dear Deborah, write solutions for alleviating suffering, such as sharing food or helping those less fortunate.

Have students keep their answers for publication in their edition of the *Ancient Israelite Times*.

Write an Editorial

Tell students that the newspaper they are writing, the *Ancient Israelite Times*, is an underground paper. That is, it will be seen by the people, but not by their leaders. Therefore, they can feel free to express their true feelings about how they are being treated in the form of an editorial.

Let the students examine the editorial page in their local newspaper. Have them explain how an editorial is different from a news article. Then have them pretend to be ancient Israelites in the time after Solomon. Encourage them to write editorials for their newspapers explaining how they feel about the political situation.

Have students keep their editorials for publication in their edition of the *Ancient Israelite Times*.

The Prophets

The divided kingdoms of Israel and Judah fell upon hard times. Israel fell to the Assyrians, and in 586 B.C. about four hundred years after Solomon's Temple was built, Nebuchadnezzar and his Babylonian warriors conquered Jerusalem. They destroyed the temple and took the Israelites into captivity. They had lost their homeland.

The Israelites wondered if God had abandoned them. But a remarkable group of people called the Prophets said that the answer was no. The Prophets said that God spoke to them and told them that the Israelites were being punished because they had broken their covenant with God by not obeying God's teachings.

The Prophets emphasized that if the Israelites would worship no other gods and act fairly toward others, the land of Israel would someday be restored.

Trace the Diaspora

The Diaspora refers to the dispersion of the Jewish people throughout Babylon, Egypt, and later, the world. Divide the class into three groups. Have one group investigate how the Jewish people were able to maintain an identity even though they were assimilated into other cultures. Students should find that basic tenets of their religious faith kept them together.

Have the second group investigate how first and second century Rome further dispersed the Jewish people throughout the world.

Have the third group trace what happened to Jewish people in World War II and tell how many of them survived almost insurmountable obstacles.

Challenge each group to present their information in the way they think best, whether it be a skit, report, or geography study.

Research Modern Israel

Assign reporters to write various pieces about the rise of the modern country of Israel. Some students can write articles telling how the country of Israel was reformed in 1948. Other students can research the conflicts and wars fought to maintain Israel. Another group can investigate the social aspects of Israel, such as life on a kibbutz. Have reporters find another student to edit their work, then save it for their edition of the *Ancient Israelite Times*.

Nebuchadnezzar worshiping

Publish the News

After students have completed their study of ancient Israel, encourge them to publish their edition of the *Ancient Israelite Times*. Gather the entire class together to brainstorm all the various tasks that it will take to publish a newspaper. List them on the chalkboard or chart paper.

After students have completed brainstorming, have them develop a plan and decide how to assign each task. Be sure to monitor their discussion and ensure that all the necessary tasks and roles are covered. Then, have the students assign roles to each member of the class, and develop a schedule for completing the final edition of the newspaper.

Assemble the Newspaper

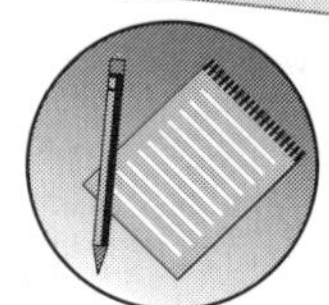

Have the reporters assemble all the news stories, pictures, interviews, advice columns, and editorials they have written. If possible, have them enter their pieces on a computer to make the newspaper look more professional. Let the students complete the *Newspaper Checklist* (page 47). When the checklist has been completed, let the students cut the masthead from the Newspaper Checklist and assemble the newspapers.

Make a Time Line

Let pairs of students make time lines showing important dates in the history of the ancient Israelites for their newspaper. The following are some important dates to include:

1900 B.C.–Abraham settles in Canaan

1250 B.C.–Moses leads the Exodus from Egypt

1000 B.C.–David becomes King of Israel

721 B.C.–Assyria conquers Israel

586 B.C.–Babylonia conquers Judah

Your students may also include dates involving other important ancient Israelites such as Isaac, Jacob, Joshua, and Saul. Have the students write the importance of each date, either above or below the time line. Tell the students to leave enough room on their time lines for illustrations.

Publish the Ancient Israelite News

Encourage reporters to share their newspapers with each other. Let them discuss and read favorite articles in the newspapers. Display the newspapers on a bulletin board. Invite students' parents and/or another class in to read and discuss the newspapers.

Newspaper Checklist

Name ______________________________

Now that you have visited the ancient Israelites as a reporter, you are ready to assemble your newspapers. Put a check mark when you finish each step.

_____ 1. Check the current drafts of all your articles. Be sure everything is exactly as you want it.

_____ 2. Let a classmate read your newspaper and suggest changes. Write the main changes here that your classmate suggests.

____

____

____

_____ 3. Type or write your newspaper carefully, including all corrections. Paste the masthead at the top of the newspaper.

_____ 4. Proofread your newspaper.

_____ Are all the sentences really sentences?

_____ Is the punctuation correct?

_____ Is the capitalization correct?

_____ Is the spelling correct?

_____ 5. Publish your newspaper by sharing it with others.

Ancient Israelite Times

Volume 1/Issue 1 721 B.C.

Bibliography

ABC: The Alef-Bet Book: The Israel Museum, Jerusalem by Florence Cassen Mayers (Abrams, 1989).

The Emergence of Man: The Israelites by the Editors of Time-Life Books (Time-Life Books, 1975).

Everyday Life in Bible Times by Melviole Bell Grosvenor, ed. (National Geographic Society, 1967).

Israel: The Land and Its People (Countries Series) by Danah Zohar (Macdonald Educational, 1977).

The Junior Encyclopedia of Israel by Harriet Sirof (Jonathan David Publishers, 1980).

Life in the Ancient World by Bart Winerr (Random House, 1961).

Lost Civilizations: The Holy Land (Time-Life Books, 1992).

Pictorial History of the Jewish People by Nathan Ausubel (Crown, 1984).

The River Jordan by Nelson Glueck (McGraw-Hill Book Company, 1968).